THE
PRODIGAL
GOD

Discussion Guide

THE
PRODIGAL
GOD

Discussion Guide

TIMOTHY KELLER

ZONDERVAN®

ZONDERVAN.com/
AUTHORTRACKER
follow your favorite authors

ZONDERVAN

The Prodigal God Discussion Guide
Copyright © 2009 by Redeemer City to City

Requests for information should be addressed to:

Zondervan, *Grand Rapids, Michigan 49530*

ISBN 978-0-310-32536-9

Interior design by Ben Fetterley

Printed in the United States of America

09 10 11 12 13 14 15 16 • 24 23 22 21 20 19 18 17 16 15 14 13 12 11 10 9 8 7 6 5 4 3 2 1

Contents

prod-i-gal / prɒdɪgəl—adjective

    1. recklessly extravagant

    2. having spent everything

LUKE 15:1 – 3, 11 – 32

[1]Now the tax collectors and "sinners" were all gathering around to hear him. [2]But the Pharisees and the teachers of the law muttered, "This man welcomes sinners and eats with them."

[3]Then Jesus told them this parable …

[11]Jesus continued: "There was a man who had two sons. [12]The younger one said to his father, 'Father, give me my share of the estate.' So he divided his property between them.

[13]"Not long after that, the younger son got together all he had, set off for a distant country and there squandered his wealth in wild living. [14]After he had spent everything, there was a severe famine in that whole country, and he began to be in need. [15]So he went and hired himself out to a citizen of that country, who sent him to his fields to feed pigs. [16]He longed to fill his stomach with the pods that the pigs were eating, but no one gave him anything.

[17]"When he came to his senses, he said, 'How many of my father's hired men have food to spare, and here I am starving to death! [18]I will set out and go back to my father and say to him: Father, I have sinned against heaven and against you. [19]I am no longer worthy to be called your son; make me like one of your hired men.' [20]So he got up and went to his father.

"But while he was still a long way off, his father saw him and was filled with compassion for him; he ran to his son, threw his arms around him and kissed him.

21"The son said to him, 'Father, I have sinned against heaven and against you. I am no longer worthy to be called your son.'

22"But the father said to his servants, 'Quick! Bring the best robe and put it on him. Put a ring on his finger and sandals on his feet. 23Bring the fattened calf and kill it. Let's have a feast and celebrate. 24For this son of mine was dead and is alive again; he was lost and is found.' So they began to celebrate.

25"Meanwhile, the older son was in the field. When he came near the house, he heard music and dancing. 26So he called one of the servants and asked him what was going on. 27'Your brother has come,' he replied, 'and your father has killed the fattened calf because he has him back safe and sound.'

28"The older brother became angry and refused to go in. So his father went out and pleaded with him. 29But he answered his father, 'Look! All these years I've been slaving for you and never disobeyed your orders. Yet you never gave me even a young goat so I could celebrate with my friends. 30But when this son of yours who has squandered your property with prostitutes comes home, you kill the fattened calf for him!'

31"'My son,' the father said, 'you are always with me, and everything I have is yours. 32But we had to celebrate and be glad, because this brother of yours was dead and is alive again; he was lost and is found.'"

INTRODUCTION

I was already pastoring a church when I was confronted with the radical idea that the gospel is neither religion nor irreligion, neither morality nor immorality, but something else entirely. We've built our vision for Redeemer Presbyterian Church in New York City and our leadership training around this concept.

This core message of the gospel is seen most clearly, I believe, in Jesus' famous parable called "The Parable of the Prodigal Son." I hope small groups and whole churches will go through this material together, because truth is most transformative when encountered in community. My prayer is that both younger brothers and elder brothers will realize that the only way home is through a prodigal God.

TIMOTHY KELLER
AUGUST 2009

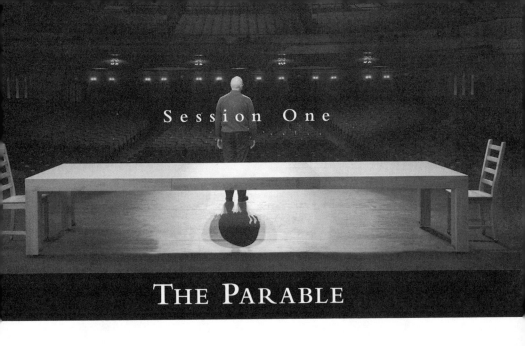

Session One

THE PARABLE

| | IN PREPARATION | |

🎵 If time allows, begin with some form of worship; for example, sing a song or read a psalm aloud.

🎵 As you begin this series, pray that God would grant you a fresh understanding of the gospel and that you and your group would be enlightened and helped by the parable.

🎵 Briefly answer the following questions aloud:
What was your reason for coming to this study?
Have you read *The Prodigal God* book?

🎵 Read Luke 15:1–3, 11–32 aloud (you can find this Scripture on pages 8–9 of this guide), then watch The Prodigal God Film (38 minutes). There is room to take notes on the following page.

DVD Notes

1. Was there anything from the DVD that was new to you or had an effect on you? Did you hear anything that raised questions in your mind?

2. Who do you identify with more, the younger brother or the elder brother? Why?

3. How close is a great feast to your idea of heaven?

4. Is there anything you would like the group to pray for you personally or as a result of what you saw on the DVD?

Pray for each other in light of your answers to question 4.

If possible, allow time for the group to have coffee or a meal together, in order to deepen relationships with one another.

Over the next five sessions we will be reading *The Prodigal God* book and discussing it together. Before the next session please read the Introduction and Chapter One. As you read, keep track of, underline, or mark (e.g., with a "?" or "!") anything you would like to discuss, question, or comment on when we next meet. There is room to take notes on the following pages.

Question 1

Your group may have questions after watching the DVD that will be answered in greater depth when they have read *The Prodigal God* book and worked through the questions in this guide. It is not necessary to answer all the comments and questions in great detail at this point.

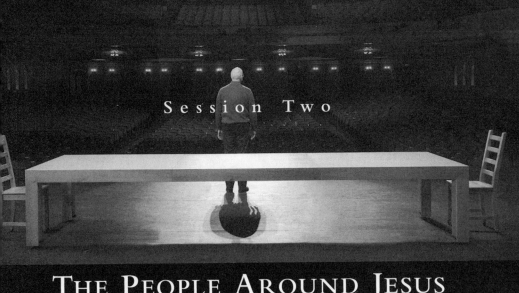

Session Two

THE PEOPLE AROUND JESUS

IN PREPARATION

- If time allows, begin with some form of worship; for example, sing a song or read a psalm aloud.

- Pray as you begin, asking God to be at work in the group.

- Watch the Session Two clip from the DVD as a recap. There is room to take notes on the following page.

"There were two groups of people around Jesus when he began to tell the parable. Tax collectors and sinners, Pharisees and teachers of the law. Now, tax collectors and sinners are like younger brothers. They've run off. They live any way they want. The Pharisees and the religious leaders are like the elder brother. They stay home, they comply, they are very good."

NOTE: Page references are to *The Prodigal God* book.

1. If you had the opportunity to read the Introduction and Chapter One of *The Prodigal God* book, what was new to you or had an effect on you? Did you read anything that raised questions in your mind?

2. Consider the audience to whom Jesus told this parable. What does that tell us about the traditional name of the parable?

   (See pages xiv and 7–9)

3. How have you seen both religious and irreligious lifestyles lead to spiritual emptiness? Share examples.

4. Can you think of other incidents from Jesus' life where he comes into conflict with the Pharisees and the teachers of the law? Why do you think they were opposed to Jesus and his teaching?

5. "Frequently the oldest sibling in a family is the parent-pleaser, the responsible one who obeys the parental standards. The younger sibling tends to be the rebel, a free spirit who prefers the company and admiration of peers. The first child grows up, takes a conventional job, and settles down near Mom and Dad, while the younger sibling goes off to live in the hip-shabby neighborhoods of New York and Los Angeles." (p. 11)

How have you observed this dynamic in your own or other families?

6. Why do you think many churches today are not attracting the broken and marginalized with Jesus' message of grace?

(See pages 15–16)

- Pray that God's Spirit will draw you closer to one another. Ask God to help you develop relationships with both elder and younger brothers.

- If possible, allow time for the group to have coffee or a meal together, in order to deepen relationships with one another.

- Before the next session please read Chapter Two and Chapter Three of *The Prodigal God* book. As you read, keep track of, underline, or mark (e.g., with a "?" or "!") anything you would like to discuss, question, or comment on when we next meet. There is room to take notes on the following pages.

Question 4

About one year into his public ministry Jesus started to clash with the Pharisees and the teachers of the law. This conflict continued over the next two years until it led finally to Jesus' arrest, illegal trial, and execution.

Some examples include:

At the healing of the paralytic man Jesus comes into conflict with the religious authorities who question his claim to be able to forgive sin. See Luke 5:17–26 (this incident is also recorded in Matt. 9:1–8 and Mark 2:1–12).

The fact that Jesus included the tax collector Levi as one of his disciples, and that he included many of Levi's friends as his followers, was utterly scandalous to the Pharisees. See Luke 5:27–31 (this incident is also recorded in Matt. 9:9–13 and Mark 2:13–17).

Jesus clashed with the religious authorities about Sabbath practices. See Luke 6:1–5 (also in Matt. 12:1–8; Mark 2:23–27); Luke 6:6–10 (also in Matt. 12:9–14; Mark 3:1–6); Luke 13:10–17; Luke 14:1–6; and John 5:1–16.

There are many incidents where the religious authorities publicly and directly question Jesus and his teaching. They question him about:

- his authority — Luke 20:1–8
  (also in Matt. 21:23–27; Mark 11:27–30)
- paying taxes to Caesar — Luke 20:20–26
  (also in Matt. 22:15–22; Mark 12:13–17)
- the resurrection of the dead — Luke 20:27–38
  (also in Matt. 22:23–32; Mark 12:18–27)
- washing of hands — Matthew 15:1–12
  (also in Mark 7:1–8)
- divorce — Matthew 19:3–9 (also in Mark 10:2–9)
- his identity — John 10:22–32.

Jesus clashed with the authorities at the temple when he called it a "den of robbers." See Luke 19:45–48 (this incident is also recorded in Matt. 21:12–17 and Mark 11:12–18).

The conflicts between Jesus and the Pharisees highlight the irreconcilable differences between gospel Christianity and the religious mentality.

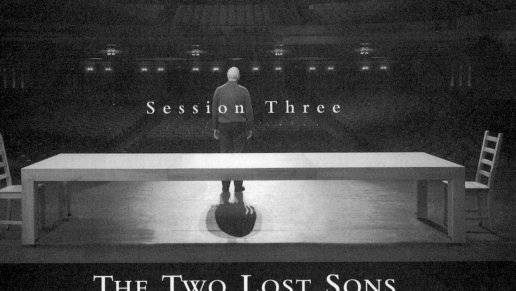

Session Three

THE TWO LOST SONS

If time allows, begin with some form of worship; for example, sing a song or read a psalm aloud.

Pray as you begin, asking God to be at work in the group.

Watch the Session Three clip from the DVD as a recap. There is room to take notes on the following page.

"You have two sons—one good, one bad. But they've both been alienated from the father. And you come to realize, they both want the father's things but not the father. They've both been using the father to get the things they really loved—which is the wealth and the status. But one has been doing it by being very, very bad and the other has been doing it by being very, very good."

NOTE: Page references are to *The Prodigal God* book.

1. If you had the opportunity to read Chapters Two and Three of *The Prodigal God* book, what was new to you or had an effect on you? Did you read anything that raised questions in your mind?

2. "There is no evil that the father's love cannot pardon and cover, there is no sin that is a match for his grace." (p. 24)

   How can this be seen in the parable, in other Bible stories, or in your own experience?

3. The younger brother believes he is no longer worthy to be called his father's son. What does that tell us about his view of what it takes to be loved and accepted? Is this view prevalent today?

4. If God's grace is absolutely free and we cannot earn it or merit it in any way, what motivation is there to live an obedient life?

5. "You can rebel against God and be alienated from him either by breaking his rules or by keeping all of them diligently." (pp. 36–37)

   Explain this statement, using examples if possible.

   (See pages 37–39)

6. How do people seek to control God through their obedience?

7. How are the younger and elder brother different? How are they alike? Use the diagram below to collect your thoughts. (See pages 33–36)

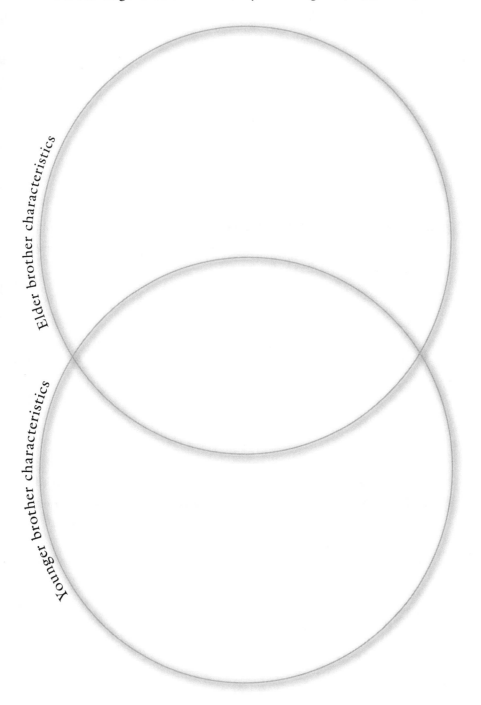

Elder brother characteristics

Younger brother characteristics

8. Where does the elder brother find his significance and happiness? Where do we tend to look for our significance and happiness? Be specific.

9. Do you agree or disagree that being an elder brother is a more spiritually desperate condition than being a younger brother? Why?
   (see pages 46–47)

10. If you asked the average person on the street to define the word "sin," what would they say? How does Jesus challenge this definition in the parable?
   (see page 43)

- Pray that you would obey God to get God himself—to resemble him, love him, know him, and delight in him.

- If possible, allow time for the group to have coffee or a meal together, in order to deepen relationships with one another.

- Before the next session please read Chapter Four of *The Prodigal God* book. As you read, keep track of, underline, or mark (e.g., with a "?" or "!") anything you would like to discuss, question, or comment on when we next meet. There is room to take notes on the following page.

Question 2

Saul was persecuting Christians when Jesus appeared to him on the road to Damascus (Acts 9:1–19).

Peter denied knowing Jesus three times (this incident is recorded in all four Gospels: Matt. 26:69–75; Mark 14:66–72; Luke 22:55–62; John 18:17–27). In Mark 14:71 we read, "He [Peter] began to call down curses on himself, and he swore to them, 'I don't know this man you're talking about.'" Jesus forgave Peter, welcomed him back as a disciple, and Peter went on to become a courageous and powerful witness for the gospel. Interestingly, of course, we would not have known about this incident had Peter himself not told what had happened. This shows that he had truly grasped the gospel of grace.

King David committed adultery with Bathsheba, then ordered the murder of her husband to cover up his sin. God sent the prophet Nathan to rebuke David, who then sought God's forgiveness (2 Sam. 11:1–12:13). David is still referred to as "a man after God's own heart."

Jonah was told by God to go to Nineveh and preach against it. Jonah went in the opposite direction. But God graciously still pursued Jonah.

Question 6

Like a taxpayer who feels he has the right to goods and services because he has paid his taxes, people — by being obedient — feel that God is obliged to reward them. As Timothy Keller says on the DVD, "There are a lot of people, there are a lot of Christians with an elder brother type of heart. If in your heart of hearts you say, 'I try very hard. I try to be obedient. I go to church. I pray. I try to serve Jesus. Therefore, God, you owe it to me to answer my prayers, to give me a relatively good life, and to take me to heaven when I die.' If that's the language of your heart, then Jesus is your model, Jesus is your example, Jesus is your boss, but he's not your savior. You're seeking to be your own savior. All your morality and all your religion, it's all just a way to get God to give you the things you really want, and they are not God himself."

Question 8

When we elevate anything to an ultimate position in our heart in order to find significance and happiness — we have an idol. An idol is anything more fundamental than God to our happiness, meaning in life, and identity. Idolatry is the inordinate desire for even something good. This means anything can become an idol, including good things.

Examples include: career; family; achievement; our independence; a political cause; material possessions; power and influence; physical attractiveness; romance; human approval; financial security; our place in a particular social circle or institution; and so on.

Please see "Additional Notes: Idolatry" beginning on page 71 at the end of this guide to further help you with this question.

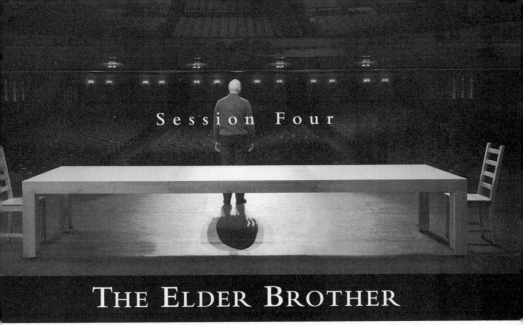

THE ELDER BROTHER

IN PREPARATION

- If time allows, begin with some form of worship; for example, sing a song or read a psalm aloud.

- Pray as you begin, asking God to be at work in the group.

- Watch the Session Four clip from the DVD as a recap. There is room to take notes on the following page.

DVD Notes

"There are two kinds of lostness. That's the reason Jesus put the elder brother in the parable. You can escape God as much through morality and religion as you can escape God through immorality and irreligion.... Elder brothers obey to get things from God, and if those things aren't forthcoming, they get very angry."

Group Discussion Questions

NOTE: Page references are to *The Prodigal God* book.

1. If you had the opportunity to read Chapter Four of *The Prodigal God* book, what was new to you or had an effect on you? Did you read anything that raised questions in your mind?

2. One way to fill out the diagram from the last session is below. Add to the elder brother characteristics from what you have read in Chapter Four of the book.

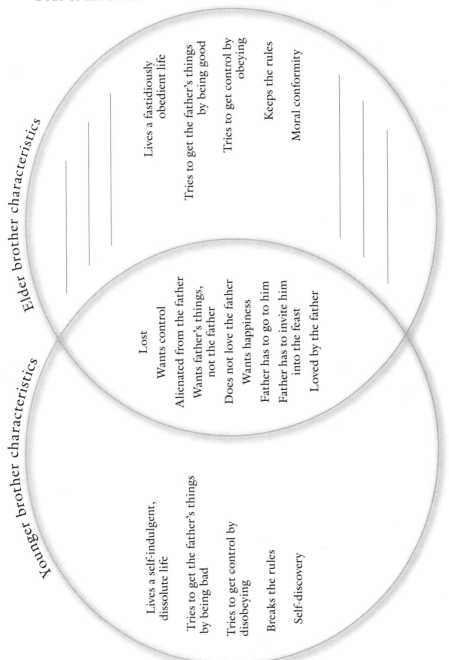

Elder brother characteristics

Lives a fastidiously obedient life

Tries to get the father's things by being good

Tries to get control by obeying

Keeps the rules

Moral conformity

Younger brother characteristics

Lost

Wants control

Alienated from the father

Wants father's things, not the father

Does not love the father

Wants happiness

Father has to go to him

Father has to invite him into the feast

Loved by the father

Lives a self-indulgent, dissolute life

Tries to get the father's things by being bad

Tries to get control by disobeying

Breaks the rules

Self-discovery

3. Fill out the following table to help you think about the relationships between the people in the parable.

How does the elder brother view ...	himself
	his brother
	his father
At the start of the parable, how does the younger brother view ...	himself
	his brother
	his father

4. "The first sign you have an elder-brother spirit is that when your life doesn't go as you want, you aren't just sorrowful but deeply angry and bitter." (p. 49)

What thoughts, feelings, and assumptions lead to such anger and bitterness?

(See pages 49–50)

5. Richard Lovelace writes, "[People] who are no longer sure that God loves and accepts them in Jesus, apart from their present spiritual achievements, are subconsciously radically insecure persons." (p. 54)

Do you agree with his assessment? Why or why not?

6. If your motivation to do good is to earn God's favor, how does this affect the goodness of the action?

(See pages 59–60)

7. How would the attitude of the elder brother make it harder for the younger brother to come home? How can you prevent this from happening in your own life and in your church?

(See pages 66–67)

8. Look back at your answers to questions 2 and 3. Do you tend to behave more like a younger brother or more like an elder brother? Were there times in your past when you behaved more like one than the other?

Look back at the lists of characteristics in question 3. Pray for younger and elder brothers of your acquaintance. Pray for yourself that you would not lapse into elder or younger brother tendencies.

If possible, allow time for the group to have coffee or a meal together, in order to deepen relationships with one another.

Before the next session please read Chapter Five of *The Prodigal God* book. As you read, keep track of, underline, or mark (e.g., with a "?" or "!") anything you would like to discuss, question, or comment on when we next meet. There is room to take notes on the following page.

Question 2

Examples of characteristics to include:

- angry
- feels superior
- an unforgiving, judgmental spirit
- joyless, fear-based compliance
- lack of assurance of the father's love (which results in an inability to deal with criticism, irresolvable guilt, and a dry prayer life)
- condescending, condemning, anxious, insecure, joyless

Session Five

THE TRUE ELDER BROTHER

- If time allows, begin with some form of worship; for example, sing a song or read a psalm aloud.

- Pray as you begin, asking God to be at work in the group.

- Watch the Session Five clip from the DVD as a recap. There is room to take notes on the following page.

"For us there is a true elder brother. There is one who loved and obeyed the father completely ... one who earned everything—he earned the robe, he earned the ring, he earned everything. But at the end of his life, what do we see? He doesn't get a royal robe, he got stripped. He doesn't get the fattened calf, he got vinegar.... And this true elder brother comes to us and says, "I did it all for you.".... In other words, salvation is absolutely free for us, but it's unbelievably costly for him."

NOTE: Page references are to *The Prodigal God* book.

1. If you had the opportunity to read Chapter Five of *The Prodigal God* book, what was new to you or had an effect on you? Did you read anything that raised questions in your mind?

2. "We will never find God unless he first seeks us." (p. 75)

   How has this been true in your own experience? Where in the Bible can we see this?

3. "To truly become Christians we must also repent of the reasons we ever did anything right. Pharisees only repent of their sins, but Christians repent for the very roots of their righteousness, too." (p. 78)

   How is this explanation different from the way most people understand repentance? How does this change the way you repent?

4. What would help you to identify the "sin under all your other sins"? (p. 78) How can you dismantle that particular sin beneath the other sins?

5. "Forgiveness always comes at a cost." (p. 83)

   How can this truth be seen in the parable? In your own experience?
   (See page 84)

6. What did it cost the father to bring his younger son home? What did it cost the elder brother? What did it cost to bring us home?
   (See pages 85 and 87)

7. If Jesus is our true elder brother, how does this change our relationship with him? Our worship? Our service? Our obedience? Our view of the future?

- Pray that you would be able to repent not only of your sins but of your righteousness as well. Thank God that we have a true elder brother in Jesus Christ who has paid the full cost to bring us home.

- If possible, allow time for the group to have coffee or a meal together, in order to deepen relationships with one another.

- Before the next session please read Chapter Six and Chapter Seven of *The Prodigal God* book. As you read, keep track of, underline, or mark (e.g., with a "?" or "!") anything you would like to discuss, question, or comment on when we next meet. There is room to take notes on the following pages.

- Next week's study is entitled "The Feast of the Father." Discuss whether you would like to throw a feast or have a special meal together at the conclusion of the week. This could be as simple as everyone bringing a special dish or going out somewhere to eat together.

Question 2

We can see this in the lives of many people in the Bible, including Abraham, Jacob, Jonah, and Paul.

This truth is also expressed in many Scripture passages. For example:

2 Corinthians 4:6
"For God, who said, 'Let light shine out of darkness,' made his light shine in our hearts to give us the light of the knowledge of the glory of God in the face of Christ."

Ephesians 2:4–9
"But because of his great love for us, God, who is rich in mercy, made us alive with Christ even when we were dead in transgressions.... For it is by grace you have been saved, through faith — and this not from yourselves, it is the gift of God — not by works, so that no one can boast."

John 6:44
"No one can come to me unless the Father who sent me draws him, and I will raise him up at the last day."

Question 4

Ask people to look for common themes that connect their choices and desires.

You could also ask them to think about what it is that most often provokes in them the strongest feelings of anger, fear, worry, envy, and so on.

It is also worth considering where their minds most easily go when they are alone with nothing else to think about.

This is a question about identifying idols of the heart. Please see "Additional Notes: Idolatry" beginning on page 71 at the end of this guide. You may want to encourage the group to read and work through the exercises to help them with this issue.

Session Six

THE FEAST OF THE FATHER

IN PREPARATION

- If time allows, begin with some form of worship; for example, sing a song or read a psalm aloud.

- Pray as you begin, asking God to be at work in the group.

- Watch the Session Six clip from the DVD as a recap. There is room to take notes on the following page.

"According to the Bible, because of our true elder brother, God is someday going to make this world home again. He's going to wipe away all death, and wipe away all suffering, and wipe away all tears, and he'll give us new bodies that run and are never weary. And it will be the ultimate feast."

GROUP DISCUSSION QUESTIONS

NOTE: Page references are to *The Prodigal God* book.

1. If you had the opportunity to read Chapters Six and Seven of *The Prodigal God* book, what was new to you or had an effect on you? Did you read anything that raised questions in your mind?

2. What positive images come to mind when you hear the word "home"?

3. How is our longing for home explained by the biblical narrative of creation ⟶ fall ⟶ redemption ⟶ restoration?

Creation (See pages 95–96)
Fall (See page 96)
Redemption (See pages 101–102)
Restoration (See pages 102–103)

4. "[Jesus'] love can become more real to you than the love of anyone else. It can delight, galvanize, and console you." (p. 108)

   How has Jesus' love delighted, galvanized, or consoled you or someone you know?

5. "The ultimate purpose of [Jesus' life and death] is not only individual salvation and pardon for sins but also the renewal of this world, the end of disease, poverty, injustice, violence, suffering, and death." (p. 110)

   In what ways can you be a part of God's plan to renew all of creation?
   (See page 112)

6. Do you agree with Martin Luther that "religion" is the default mode of the human heart? In what ways can "religion" be an obstacle for us as we seek to obey Christ?
   (See page 115)

7. "Behavioral compliance to rules without heart-change will be superficial and fleeting." (p. 119)

How have you found this to be true in your own experience? How then is real, lasting change possible?

(See pages 118–119)

8. "[T]here is no way you will be able to grow spiritually apart from a deep involvement in a community of other believers." (p. 125)

Why is this true?

(See page 127)

9. The book mentions four things we need in order to have a foretaste of future salvation now—prayer, service to others, changes in our inner nature through the gospel, and healed relationships that Christ can give. Which of these do you hunger for the most, and why?

10. In ancient times a feast had more dimensions to it than merely eating. It was a time to sing, dance, reunite with long-lost friends, renew relationships, celebrate community, and so on. What joys do you most anticipate at the feast of the Father?

In Closing

Use your answers to question 10 to thank God for the amazing future he has in store for you. Pray that the gospel would continue to transform your heart and your community.

If possible, allow time for the group to have a meal or feast together.

As this completes the six-session study, consider meeting together soon to watch the film *Babette's Feast*. This movie ends with a feast and is a vivid portrayal of the two ways to live, as described by the parable.

FURTHER READING

Ferguson, Sinclair. *Children of the Living God* (Banner of Truth, 1989).

Horton, Michael. *Putting Amazing Back into Grace*, 2nd ed. (Baker, 2002).

Keller, Timothy. Sermon: "Sin as Self-Righteousness" (available from www.redeemer.com).

Keller, Timothy. Sermon Series: "The Fellowship of Grace" (available from www.redeemer.com).

Keller, Timothy. Sermon: "Removing Idols of the Heart" (available from www.redeemer.com).

Lovelace, Richard F. *Renewal as a Way of Life: A Guidebook for Spiritual Growth* (Wipf & Stock, 2002).

Plantinga, Cornelius. *Not the Way It's Supposed to Be: A Breviary of Sin* (Wm. B. Eerdmans, 1995).

Ramachandra, Vinoth. *Gods That Fail* (InterVarsity Press, 1997).

Stevenson, Leslie. *Seven Theories of Human Nature*, 2nd ed. (Oxford University Press, USA, 1987).

Yancey, Philip. *The Jesus I Never Knew* (Zondervan, 1995).

ACKNOWLEDGMENTS

The Prodigal God Discussion Guide and DVD were developed from material by Timothy Keller. All quotations from *The Prodigal God* book are used by kind permission of Penguin Dutton, which published the book in 2008.

We are deeply grateful to: Sue Fletcher, Santino Stoner, Brett VanTil, David Wenzel, and the team at Dot&Cross for their masterful production of the film; John Raymond, Greg Clouse, Mike Cook, Ben Fetterley, Rob Monacelli, Robin Phillips, and the rest of the Zondervan team for their creative collaboration; Kathy Keller and Sam Shammas for developing the film script and this study guide; and Scott Kauffmann, whose dedication and passion made the entire project a reality.

We are also grateful to all those who offered ideas and suggestions, especially to Janet Ballard and John Tinnin.

ADDITIONAL NOTES: IDOLATRY

The following extract is taken from the eight-week small group study *Gospel in Life*. It is used by permission of Redeemer Presbyterian Church and Redeemer City to City. See www.gospelinlife.com for more information.

"A careful reading of the Old and New Testaments shows that idolatry is nothing like the crude, simplistic picture that springs to mind of an idol sculpture in some distant country. As the main category to describe unbelief, the idea is highly sophisticated, drawing together the complexities of motivation in individual psychology, the social environment, and also the unseen world. Idols are not just on pagan altars, but in well-educated human hearts and minds (Ezekiel 14). The apostle Paul associates the dynamics of human greed, lust, craving, and coveting with idolatry (Ephesians 5:5; Colossians 3:5). The Bible does not allow us to marginalize idolatry to the fringes of life... it is found on center stage".[1]

The quote above indicates the pervasiveness of idolatry in the Old and New Testaments. Opposite is an overview of idolatry throughout the Bible. See if you agree with the conclusion above that "the Bible does not allow us to marginalize idolatry to the fringes of life... it is found on center stage."

Idolatry in the Old Testament

In the beginning—idolatry

In the beginning, human beings were made to (1) worship and serve God, and then (2) to rule over all created things in God's name (Gen.1:26–28). Instead, we fell into sin. When Paul sums up the fall of humanity into sin, he does so by describing it in terms of idolatry. He says we refused to give God glory (i.e., to make him the most important thing) and instead chose certain parts of creation to glorify in his stead: "[They] exchanged the glory of the immortal God...and worshiped and served created things rather than the Creator" (Rom.1:23–25). In short, we reversed the originally intended order. Human beings came to 1) worship and serve created things, and therefore 2) the created things came to rule over them.

The Law—against idols

The great sin of the Mosaic period is the making of a golden calf (Ex. 32). The Ten Commandments' first two and most basic laws are against idolatry. The first commandment prohibits worshipping other gods; the second commandment prohibits worshipping God idolatrously, as we want him to be. After God's code of covenant behavior is given in Exodus 20-23, there is a summary warning against making a covenant with other gods (Ex. 23:24) because they "snare" you (Ex. 23:33). Exodus does not envision any third option. We will either worship God, or we will worship some created thing (an idol). Every human personality, every human community, and every human thought-form will be based on some ultimate concern or some ultimate allegiance to something. Luther put it like this:

> [A]ll those who do not at all times trust God and do not in all their works or sufferings, life and death, trust in His favor, grace and good-will, but seek His favor in other things or in themselves, do not keep this [First] Commandment, and practise real idolatry, even if they were to do the works of all the other Commandments, and in addition had all the prayers, fasting, obedience, patience, and chastity of all the saints combined. For the chief work is not present, without which all the others are nothing but mere sham, show and pretence...[2]

[1] Richard Keyes, "The Idol Factory" in *No God but God: Breaking with the Idols of Our Age*, ed. Os Guinness & John Seel (Chicago: Moody Press, 1992), 31.
[2] Martin Luther, *A Treatise On Good Works*, 1520 (Kessinger Publishing), Part X, pg. 18.

The Psalms—praying against idols

In the Psalms, the prayers of the people are not only toward God, but also against idols. Psalm 24:3–4 says, "Who may ascend the hill of the Lord? Who may stand in his holy place? He who has clean hands and a pure heart, who does not lift up his soul to an idol...."

The Prophets—polemic against idols

Isaiah, Jeremiah, and Ezekiel leveled an enormous polemic against the worship of idols. First, they said, an idol is empty, nothing, powerless. An idol is nothing but what we ourselves have made, the work of our own hands (Isa. 2:8; Jer. 1:16). Thus, an idol is something we make in our image. It is only, in a sense, worshiping ourselves, or a reflection of our own sensibility (Isa. 44:10–13).

Second, an idol is, paradoxically, a spiritually dangerous power that saps you of all power. This is a triple paradox. Idols are powerless things that are all about getting power. The more you seek power through them, however, the more they drain you of strength. Idols bring about terrible spiritual blindness of heart and mind (Isa. 44:9, 18), and the idolater is self-deluded through a web of lies (Isa. 44:20). Also, idols bring about slavery. Jeremiah likens our relationship to idols as a love-addicted person to his or her lover (Jer. 2:25). Idols poison the heart into complete dependence on them (Isa. 44:17); they completely capture our hearts (Ezek. 14:1-5). They become our lord, as Rebecca Pippert observes.

> Whatever controls us is our lord. The person who seeks power is controlled by power. The person who seeks acceptance is controlled by the people he or she wants to please. We do not control ourselves. We are controlled by the lord of our life.[3]

Idolatry in the New Testament

The word "epithumiai," meaning "inordinate desires," is very common in the New Testament and has strong links to the idea of idolatry. Every sin is rooted in the inordinate desire for something, which comes because we are trusting in an idol rather than in Christ for our righteousness or salvation. This is why the word "epithumiai" shows up in so many of the New Testament sections that treat Christian character, such as the "fruit of the Spirit" passage (see Galatians 5:22–26). David Powlison explains.

> If "idolatry" is the characteristic and summary Old Testament word for our drift from God, then "desires" (*epithumiai*) is the characteristic and summary New Testament word for the same drift.[4] Both are shorthand for *the* problem of human beings.... [T]he New Testament merges the concept of idolatry and the concept of inordinate, life-ruling desires. Idolatry becomes a problem of the heart, a metaphor for human lust, craving, yearning, and greedy demand.[5]

Romans 1:18–25

This passage tells us that the reason we make idols is because we want to control our lives, though we know that we owe God everything. "For although they knew God, they neither glorified him as God nor gave thanks to him" (v. 21). Verse 25 describes the strategy for control: taking created things and setting our hearts on them and building our lives around them. Since we need to worship something because of how we are created, we cannot eliminate God without creating God-substitutes. "They exchanged the truth of God for a lie" (Rom. 1:25). Verses 21 and 25 tell us the two results of idolatry: (1) "their thinking became futile and their foolish hearts were darkened," and (2) they "worshiped and served created things."

Galatians 4:8–9

Paul is saying, "Don't go back to idolatry." Paul reminds the Galatians that they had once been enslaved "to those who by nature are not gods. But...how is it that you are turning back to those weak and miserable principles? Do you wish to be enslaved by them all over again?" (Gal. 4:8–9). The danger to the Galatians is following those who are telling them to be circumcised and who are trying to lure them into moralism, thereby clouding their understanding of justification by faith alone. How, then, can Paul talk of this as a return to idolatry? The implications are significant. If anything but Christ is your justification, you are falling into idolatry. If you sacrifice to a statue or seek to merit heaven through conscientious morality, you are setting up something besides God as your ultimate hope, and it will enslave you.

---

[3] Rebecca Manley Pippert, *Out of the Saltshaker & into the World* (Downers Grove, IL: InterVarsity Press, 1979), 53.

[4] "See such summary statements by Paul, Peter, John, and James as Galatians 5:16ff; Ephesians 2:3 & 4:22; 1 Peter 2:11 & 4:2; 1 John 2:16; James 1:14f, where *epithumiai* is the catch-all for what is wrong with us." Footnote taken from the article below.

[5] David Powlison, "Idols of the Heart and 'Vanity Fair'," *The Journal of Biblical Counseling*, Volume 13, Number 2 (Winter 1995): 36.

1 John 5:21

The last verse of 1 John is, "Dear children, keep yourselves from idols." John has not mentioned idolatry by name once in the entire letter, so we have to conclude one of two things. Either he is now, in the very last sentence, changing the whole subject, or he is summarizing all he has been saying in the epistle about living in the light (holiness), love, and truth. The latter seems more reasonable—and these implications are also significant. John, in one brief statement, is expressing in negative terms what he had spent the whole letter putting in the positive. This must mean that the only way to walk in holiness, love, and truth is to keep free from idols. They are mutually exclusive. Underlying any failure to walk in holiness is some form of idolatry.

Identifying your idols

Why do we lie, or fail to love, or break our promises, or live selfishly? Of course, the general answer is "Because we are weak and sinful," but the specific answer is always that there is something besides Jesus Christ that we feel we must have to be happy, something that is more important to our heart than God, something that is enslaving our heart through inordinate desires. The key to change (and even to self-understanding) is always to identify the idols of the heart. Thomas Oden writes,

> Every self exists in relation to values perceived as making life worth living. A *value* is anything good in the created order—any idea, relation, object or person in which one has an interest, from which one derives significance... These values compete.... In time one is prone to choose a *center of value* by which other values are judged. When a finite value has been elevated to centrality and imagined as a final source of meaning, then one has chosen...a god.... One has a god when a finite value is...viewed as that without which one cannot receive life joyfully.[6]

We often don't go deeply enough to analyze our idol-structures. For example, "money" is of course an idol; yet, in another sense, money can be sought to satisfy other very different idols. That is, some people want money in order to control their world and life (such people usually don't spend their money, but save it), while others want money for access to social circles and for making themselves beautiful and attractive (such people do spend their money on themselves). The same goes for sex. Some people use sex in order to get power over others, others in order to feel approved and loved, and others just for pleasure or comfort. Richard Keyes notes,

> All sorts of things are potential idols.... If this is so, how do we determine when something is becoming or has become an idol?... As soon as our loyalty to anything leads us to disobey God, we are in danger of making it an idol.... An idol can be a physical object, a property, a person, an activity, a role, an institution, a hope, an image, an idea, a pleasure, a hero...
>
> • Work, a commandment of God, can become an idol if it is pursued so exclusively that responsibilities to one's family are ignored.
>
> • Family, an institution of God Himself, can become an idol if one is so preoccupied with the family that no one outside of one's own family is cared for.
>
> • Being well-liked, a perfectly legitimate hope, becomes an idol if the attachment to it means that one never risks disapproval.[7]

✌ *Answer these questions, which will begin to help you identify your idols.*

1. What is my greatest nightmare? What do I worry about most?

2. What, if I failed or lost it, would cause me to feel that I did not even want to live? What keeps me going?

3. What do I rely on or comfort myself with when things go badly or become difficult?

[6] Thomas C. Oden, *Two Worlds: Notes on the Death of Modernity in America & Russia* (Downers Grove, IL: InterVarsity Press, 1992), 94-95.
[7] Richard Keyes, "The Idol Factory" in *No God but God: Breaking with the Idols of Our Age*, ed. Os Guinness & John Seel (Chicago: Moody Press, 1992), 32-33.

4. What do I think most easily about? What does my mind go to when I am free? What pre-occupies me?

5. What makes me feel the most self-worth? What am I the proudest of?

6. What do I really want and expect out of life? What would really make me happy?

✂️ *Read through the statements opposite and circle the thoughts that most resonate with you.*

"Life only has meaning/I only have worth if… I have power and influence over others." (Power idolatry)

"Life only has meaning/I only have worth if… I am loved and respected by _____." (Approval idolatry)

"Life only has meaning/I only have worth if…
I have this kind of pleasure experience, a particular quality of life." (Comfort idolatry)

"Life only has meaning/I only have worth if…
I am able to get mastery over my life in the area of _____." (Control idolatry)

"Life only has meaning/I only have worth if… people are dependent on me and need me." (Helping idolatry)

"Life only has meaning/I only have worth if…
someone is there to protect me and keep me safe." (Dependence idolatry)

"Life only has meaning/I only have worth if…
I am completely free from obligations or responsibilities to take care of someone." (Independence idolatry)

"Life only has meaning/I only have worth if… I am highly productive and getting a lot done." (Work idolatry)

"Life only has meaning/I only have worth if…
I am being recognized for my accomplishments, and I am excelling in my career." (Achievement idolatry)

"Life only has meaning/I only have worth if…
I have a certain level of wealth, financial freedom, and very nice possessions." (Materialism idolatry)

"Life only has meaning/I only have worth if…
I am adhering to my religion's moral codes and accomplished in its activities." (Religion idolatry)

"Life only has meaning/I only have worth if…
this one person is in my life and happy to be there, and/or happy with me." (Individual person idolatry)

"Life only has meaning/I only have worth if…
I feel I am totally independent of organized religion and am living by a self-made morality." (Irreligion idolatry)

"Life only has meaning/I only have worth if…
my race and culture is ascendant and recognized as superior." (Racial/cultural idolatry)

"Life only has meaning/I only have worth if…
a particular social grouping or professional grouping or other group lets me in." (Inner ring idolatry)

"Life only has meaning/I only have worth if…
my children and/or my parents are happy and happy with me." (Family idolatry)

"Life only has meaning/I only have worth if… Mr. or Ms. 'Right' is in love with me." (Relationship idolatry)

"Life only has meaning/I only have worth if…
I am hurting, in a problem; only then do I feel worthy of love or able to deal with guilt." (Suffering idolatry)

"Life only has meaning/I only have worth if…
my political or social cause is making progress and ascending in influence or power." (Ideology idolatry)

"Life only has meaning/I only have worth if… I have a particular kind of look or body image." (Image idolatry)

✎ If you circled one of the first four on the list overleaf, the following table may help you think through some of the issues involved:

What we seek	You will feel	Greatest nightmare	Others often feel	Problem emotion
POWER (Success, winning, influence)	Burdened	Humiliation	Used	Anger
APPROVAL (Affirmation, love, relationships)	Less independence	Rejection	Smothered	Cowardice
COMFORT (Privacy, lack of stress, freedom)	Reduced productivity	Stress, demands	Hurt	Boredom
CONTROL (Self-discipline, certainty, standards)	Loneliness	Uncertainty	Condemned	Worry

✎ Now that you've answered the questions above, look for common themes. What things tend to be too important to you? What are your idols?

Displacing your idols

Three approaches to personal change appear below.

The "moralizing" approach

Basic analysis: Your problem is that you are doing wrong. Repent!

This approach focuses on behavior, but doesn't go deeply enough. We must find out the *why* of our behavior. Why do I find I want to do the wrong things? What inordinate desires are drawing me to do so? What are the idols and false beliefs behind them?

To simply tell an unhappy person (or yourself) to "Repent and change behavior" is insufficient, because the lack of self-control is coming from a belief that says, "Even if you live up to moral standards but don't have this particular thing that you treasure, you are still a failure."

You must replace this belief by repenting for the one sin beneath it all—your particular idolatry.

The "psychologizing" approach

Basic analysis: Your problem is that you don't see that God loves you as you are. Rejoice!

This approach focuses on feelings, which seem to be "deeper" than behaviors, but it also fails to go deeply enough. We must also find out the *why* of our feelings. Why do I have such strong feelings of despair (or fear, or anger) when this or that happens? What are the inordinate desires that are being frustrated? What are the idols and false beliefs behind them?

To simply tell an unhappy person (or yourself) that "God loves you, so rejoice!" is insufficient, because the unhappiness is coming from a belief that says, "Even if God loves you but you don't have this particular thing that you treasure, you are still a failure."

You must replace this belief by repenting for the one sin beneath it all—your particular idolatry.

The "gospel" approach

Basic analysis: Your problem is that you are looking to something besides Christ for your happiness. You have been worshiping an idol and rejecting the true God. Repent and rejoice!

This approach confronts a person with the real sin underlying the sins and behind the bad feelings. Our problem is that we have given ourselves over to idols. Every idol-system is a way of our-works-salvation, and thus it keeps us "under the law."

Paul tells us that the bondage of sin is broken when we come out from under the law—when we begin to believe the gospel of Christ's-work-salvation. Only when we realize in a new way that we are righteous in Christ does the idol's power over us break. "Sin shall not be your master, because you are not under law, but under grace" (Rom. 6:14).

You will only be "under grace" and free from the controlling effects of idols to the degree that you have both (1) repented of your idols and (2) rested and rejoiced in the saving work and love of Christ instead.

To replace idols, you must learn to rejoice in the particular thing Jesus provides that replaces that particular idol of your heart. Whenever you see your heart in the grip of some kind of disobedience or misery, some temptation, anxiety, anger, etc., always ask, (1) How are these effects being caused by an inordinate hope for someone or something to give me what only Jesus can really give me? and (2) How does Christ give me so much more fully and graciously and suitably the very things I am looking for elsewhere? Next, rejoice and consider what he has done and what he has given you. Thomas Chalmers understood this when he wrote,

> It is seldom that any of our [bad habits or flaws] are made to disappear by a mere process of natural extinction. At least, it is very seldom that this is done through the instrumentality of reasoning...[or by] the mere force of mental determination. But what cannot be thus destroyed may be dispossessed—and one taste may be made to give way to another, and to lose its power entirely as the reigning affection

of the mind.... [T]he heart['s]...desire for having some one object or other, this is unconquerable.... [T]he only way to dispossess [the heart] of an old affection is by the expulsive power of a new one.... It is...when admitted into the number of God's children, through the faith that is in Jesus Christ, [that] the spirit of adoption is poured upon us—it is then that the heart, brought under the mastery of one great and predominant affection, is delivered from the tyranny of its former desires, and is the only way in which deliverance is possible.[8]

Look at the answers you gave in the "Identifying your idols" section. Pray that you would be able to repent of your idols and rejoice in the saving love of Jesus; that you would look only to Christ for your salvation and identity; and that you would be able to break the power your idols hold over you. The following may help you to pray.

Name the idols

In prayer, name these things to God. Sample prayer language:

"Lord, these are the things I have built my life and heart around...."

Repent of the idols

Recognize how weak and poor they are (in themselves). In prayer, confess that these things are good, but finite and weak, and praise God for being the only source of what you need. Sample prayer language:

"Lord, this is a good thing, yet why have I made it so absolute? What is this compared to you? If I have you, I don't have to have this. This cannot love me and help me as you do. This is not my life—Jesus is my life. This is not my righteousness and worthiness. It cannot give me that—but you can and have!"

Recognize how dangerous they are (to you). Idols enslave, and they will never be satisfied. Realize how they increasingly destroy you. In prayer, confess that these things are lethal, and ask a strong God for his help. Sample prayer language:

"Lord, why am I giving this so much power over me? If I keep doing it, it will strangle me. I don't have to do so—I will not do so any longer. This will not be my master. You are my only King."

[8] Thomas Chalmers, "The Expulsive Power of a New Affection" in *The Protestant Pulpit*, ed. Andrew W. Blackwood (New York: Abingdon Press, 1947), 52-56.

Recognize how grievous they are (to Christ). Realize that when you pine after idols (in your anger, fear, despondency), you are saying, "Lord, you are not enough. This is more beautiful, fulfilling, and sweet to my taste than you. You are negotiable, but this is not." In prayer, admit how deeply you have grieved and de-valued Jesus, and ask forgiveness. Sample prayer language:

> "Lord, I see how repulsive idolizing this mere idol really is. In yearning after this, I was trampling on your love for me. I realize now my lack of thankfulness, my lack of grateful joy for what you have done for me."

Rejoice in Christ

The following prayers will not affect you unless—as you pray and praise and meditate—the Spirit inscribes the gospel truths on your heart. It is not only important to spend time repenting and rejoicing in fixed times of solitude and prayer; you must also "catch" your heart when it begins falling into idolatry during the day, and you must draw on your hard work of reflection by learning to quickly repent/rejoice your heart into shape on the spot.

Sample rejoicing prayer for times of temptation:

> "Lord, only in your presence is fullness of joy and pleasures forever more (Ps. 16:11), yet here am I trying to find comfort in something else. This thing I am tempted by is just a pleasure that will wear off so soon. It is a sham and cheat, while your pleasure, though it may start small, will grow on and on forever (Prov. 4:18). Please remove my idol of pleasure, which can never give me the pleasure I need."

Meditate on John 6, verses 5–13 and 32–40.

Sample rejoicing prayer for times of anxiety:

> "Lord, I live by your sheer grace. That means though I don't deserve to have things go right, yet I know you are working them all out for good (Rom. 8:28), because you love me in Christ. My security in life is based neither on luck nor hard work, but on your gracious love for me. You have counted every hair on my head (Matt. 10:30-31) and every tear down my cheeks (Ps. 56:8). You love me far more and better than anyone else loves me, or than I love myself. Please remove my idol of security, which can never give me the security I need."

Meditate on Luke 8:22-25 and Mark 4:35-41.

Sample rejoicing prayer for times of anger:

> "Lord, when I forget the gospel I become impatient and judgmental toward others. I forget that you have been infinitely patient with me over the years. You are 'slow to anger and rich in love' (Ps. 145:8). When I am anything other than tender-hearted and compassionate to people around me, I am like the unmerciful servant, who, having been forgiven an infinite debt, is hard toward his fellow debtor (Matt. 18:21-35). Please remove the idol of power—the need to get my own way—which is making me so hard toward these people."

Meditate on Matthew 26:36-46.

Sample rejoicing prayer for times of struggling with rejection and a sense of worthlessness:

> "Lord, when I forget the gospel I become dependent on the smiles and evaluation of others. I let them sit in judgment on me, and then I hear all their criticism as a condemnation of my very being. But you have said there is no condemnation for me now (Rom. 8:1). You delight and sing over me (Zeph. 3:14-17). You see me as a beauty (Col. 1:22). Let me be so satisfied with your love (Ps. 90:14) that I no longer respond to people in fear of displeasing them, but in love, committed to what is best for them. Please remove my idol of approval, which can never give me the approval I need."

Meditate on John 15:9-17 and 17:13-26.

You may have other idols besides the four mentioned above. For example, you may have a particular problem with guilt over the past, or with boredom in general, and so on. Follow the same pattern you see above: How does Jesus particularly provide what the idol cannot? Pray to him, thanking him for his provision, and find some passage of Scripture in which he very visibly and concretely demonstrates this gift or quality. Meditate on it.

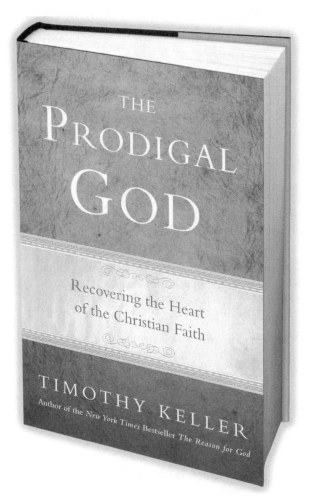

Share Your Thoughts

With the Author: Your comments will be forwarded to the author when you send them to *zauthor@zondervan.com*.

With Zondervan: Submit your review of this book by writing to *zreview@zondervan.com*.

Free Online Resources at

www.zondervan.com

Zondervan AuthorTracker: Be notified whenever your favorite authors publish new books, go on tour, or post an update about what's happening in their lives.

Daily Bible Verses and Devotions: Enrich your life with daily Bible verses or devotions that help you start every morning focused on God.

Free Email Publications: Sign up for newsletters on fiction, Christian living, church ministry, parenting, and more.

Zondervan Bible Search: Find and compare Bible passages in a variety of translations at www.zondervanbiblesearch.com.

Other Benefits: Register yourself to receive online benefits like coupons and special offers, or to participate in research.